Over and Under

A Sesame Street Guessing Game

Mari Schuh

Lerner Publications ◆ Minneapolis

Join your favorite *Sesame Street* friends in a guessing game and learn about words that describe where things are. In the **Sesame Street® Directional Words** series, learning is fun for everyone in the neighborhood—especially when you're with your fabulous, furry friends!

Sincerely,
The Editors at Sesame Workshop

Table of Contents

Over and Under

Over and **under** help us say where something or someone is.

Elmo jumped **over** a puddle!

Something is **over** you if it is above you or on top of something else.

Birds fly **over** the flowers.

If something is below you, then it is **under** you.

When I dance on the rug, the rug is **under** me.

Can You Guess?

Let's play a game to learn more about **over** and **under**.

Elmo love games and learning!

Friends are jumping rope.

Are they jumping **over** or **under** the rope?

They jump **over** the rope.

It's fun to jump rope!

It is raining. Grover wants to stay dry.

Does he stand **over** or **under** the umbrella?

Grover stands **under** the umbrella.

Hello, everybody! No raindrops on me!

It's time to go outside! Friends are putting on their coats.

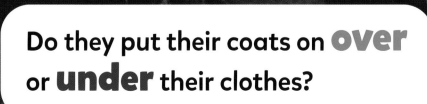

Do they put their coats on **over** or **under** their clothes?

They put their coats on **over** their clothes.

Let's go outside to play!

It's time for breakfast!

Do you push your chair **over**
or **under** the table?

You push the chair **under** the table.

It's time to have a great day!

Elmo wants to get cozy for bedtime.

Is he **under** the blanket or **over** the blanket?

Elmo is **under** the blanket.

Baby David likes to be cozy **under** the blanket too!

We can use **over** and **under** to say where things or people are. What do you see that is **over** or **under** something else?

The bench is **under** the tree!

Zoe is having a fun day at the park. Where would Zoe be if she was **under** the jungle gym bars?

Where would Zoe have to stand to be **over** the water?

Picture Glossary

bedtime: when someone goes to bed

cozy: comfortable

rug: a piece of material used to cover part of a floor

umbrella: a cloth stretched over a folding frame with a handle

Read More

Banks, Rosie. *I Know Over and Under.* New York: Gareth Stevens, 2023.

Culliford, Amy. *Over and Under.* New York: Crabtree, 2022.

Kenan, Tessa. *Over and Under.* Minneapolis: Jump!, 2019.

Index

Photo Acknowledgments

Image credits: FluxFactory/E+/Getty Images (puddle), p. 4; kavram/iStock/Getty Images, p. 5; Cavan Images/Getty Images, pp. 6, 19, 22 (bottom left); FatCamera/iStock/Getty Images, p. 9; IrenD/Shutterstock (raindrops), p. 11; Sara Monika/Image Source/Getty Images, pp. 13, 22 (top right); Indeed/ABSODELS/Getty Images, p. 15; kali9/E+/Getty Images, p. 20; Ivanna Lopatska/EyeEm/Getty Images, p. 21; JGI/Jamie Grill/Tetra Images/Getty Images, p. 22 (top left); Moyo Studio/E+/Getty Images, p. 22 (top right); Kamonrat Meunklad/EyeEm/Getty Images, p. 22 (bottom right).
Cover: Steve Satushek/The Image Bank/Getty Images (right); skynesher/E+/Getty Images (left).

For the students at St. John Vianney School in Fairmont, Minnesota

Lerner Publications Company
An imprint of Lerner Publishing Group, Inc.
241 First Avenue North
Minneapolis, MN 55401 USA

For reading levels and more information, look up this title at www.lernerbooks.com.

Main body text set in Mikado.
Typeface provided by HVD.

Designer: Laura Otto Rinne **Photo Editor:** Annie Zheng
Lerner team: Martha Kranes

Library of Congress Cataloging-in-Publication Data

Names: Schuh, Mari C., 1975- author.
Title: Over and under : a Sesame Street guessing game / Mari Schuh.
Description: Minneapolis : Lerner Publications, [2023] | Series: Sesame street directional words | Includes bibliographical references and index. | Audience: Ages 4–8. | Audience: Grades K–1. | Summary: "Readers join their friends from Sesame Street to learn the meaning of over and under. A fun guessing game with kid-friendly examples engages readers"– Provided by publisher.
Identifiers: LCCN 2022037612 (print) | LCCN 2022037613 (ebook) | ISBN 9781728486758 (library binding) | ISBN 9798765601150 (ebook)
Subjects: LCSH: Orientation–Juvenile literature. | Guessing games–Juvenile literature.
Classification: LCC BF299.O7 S383 2023 (print) | LCC BF299.O7 (ebook) | DDC 155–dc23/eng/20221116

LC record available at https://lccn.loc.gov/2022037612
LC ebook record available at https://lccn.loc.gov/2022037613

Manufactured in the United States of America
1-52620-50794-1/26/2023